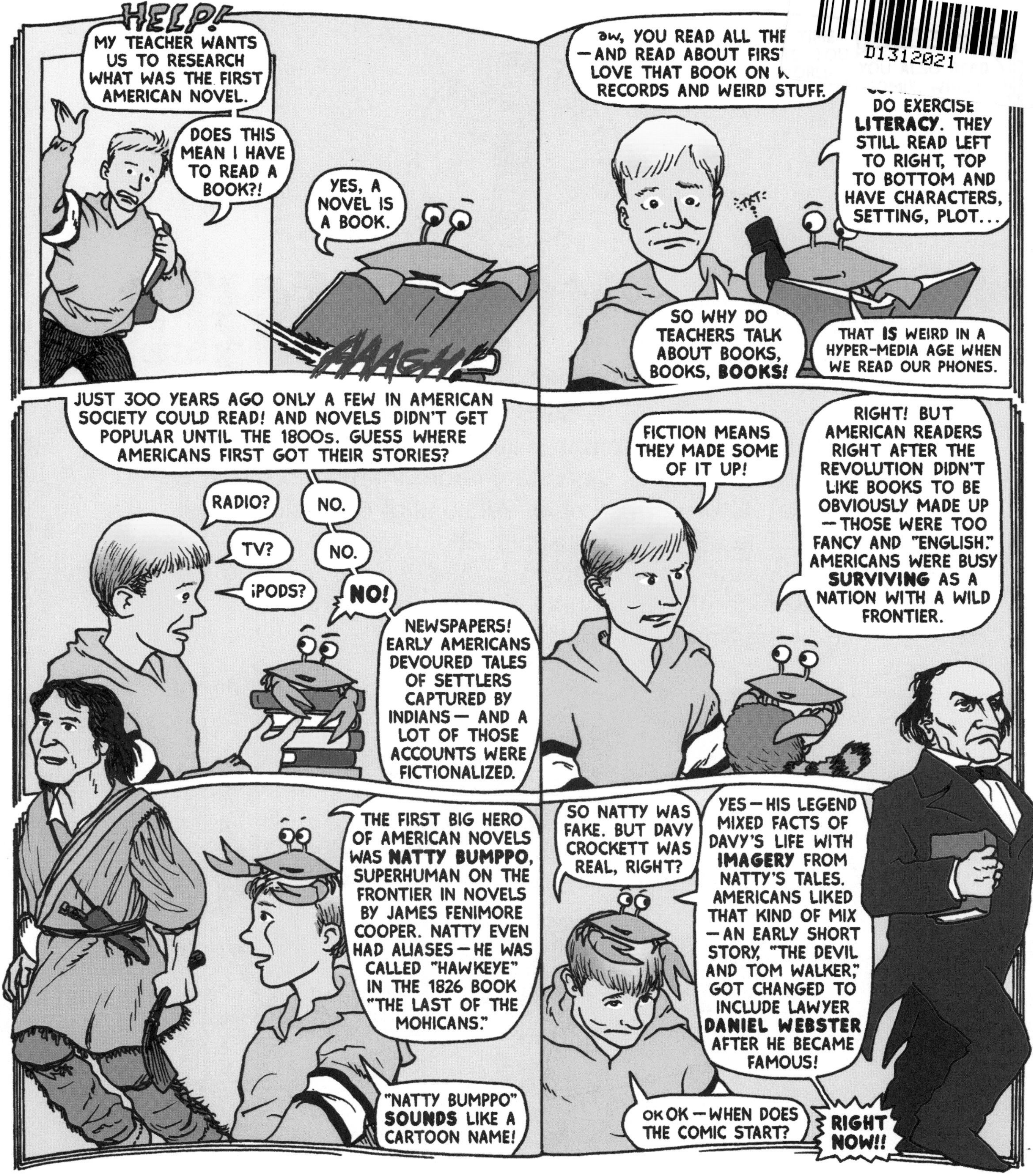
HELP!
MY TEACHER WANTS US TO RESEARCH WHAT WAS THE FIRST AMERICAN NOVEL.
DOES THIS MEAN I HAVE TO READ A BOOK?!
YES, A NOVEL IS A BOOK.
AAAGH!
aw, YOU READ ALL THE
—AND READ ABOUT FIRST
LOVE THAT BOOK ON
RECORDS AND WEIRD STUFF.
DO EXERCISE LITERACY. THEY STILL READ LEFT TO RIGHT, TOP TO BOTTOM AND HAVE CHARACTERS, SETTING, PLOT...
SO WHY DO TEACHERS TALK ABOUT BOOKS, BOOKS, BOOKS!
THAT IS WEIRD IN A HYPER-MEDIA AGE WHEN WE READ OUR PHONES.
JUST 300 YEARS AGO ONLY A FEW IN AMERICAN SOCIETY COULD READ! AND NOVELS DIDN'T GET POPULAR UNTIL THE 1800s. GUESS WHERE AMERICANS FIRST GOT THEIR STORIES?
RADIO?
NO.
TV?
NO.
iPODS?
NO!
NEWSPAPERS! EARLY AMERICANS DEVOURED TALES OF SETTLERS CAPTURED BY INDIANS— AND A LOT OF THOSE ACCOUNTS WERE FICTIONALIZED.
FICTION MEANS THEY MADE SOME OF IT UP!
RIGHT! BUT AMERICAN READERS RIGHT AFTER THE REVOLUTION DIDN'T LIKE BOOKS TO BE OBVIOUSLY MADE UP —THOSE WERE TOO FANCY AND "ENGLISH." AMERICANS WERE BUSY SURVIVING AS A NATION WITH A WILD FRONTIER.
THE FIRST BIG HERO OF AMERICAN NOVELS WAS NATTY BUMPPO, SUPERHUMAN ON THE FRONTIER IN NOVELS BY JAMES FENIMORE COOPER. NATTY EVEN HAD ALIASES—HE WAS CALLED "HAWKEYE" IN THE 1826 BOOK "THE LAST OF THE MOHICANS."
"NATTY BUMPPO" SOUNDS LIKE A CARTOON NAME!
SO NATTY WAS FAKE. BUT DAVY CROCKETT WAS REAL, RIGHT?
YES—HIS LEGEND MIXED FACTS OF DAVY'S LIFE WITH IMAGERY FROM NATTY'S TALES. AMERICANS LIKED THAT KIND OF MIX —AN EARLY SHORT STORY, "THE DEVIL AND TOM WALKER," GOT CHANGED TO INCLUDE LAWYER DANIEL WEBSTER AFTER HE BECAME FAMOUS!
OK OK—WHEN DOES THE COMIC START?
RIGHT NOW!!

CHAPTER 1

JOHNNY APPLESEED

After the United States won its indepedence as a nation, **John Chapman** was one of the first real Americans to pick up a story larger than himself. **Legends** are also simpler versions of the historical fact. The real "Johnny Appleseed" didn't just wander the woods flinging apple seeds around; he lived a careful, thoughtful life that knitted the growing American frontier together . . .

CHESTER THE CRAB | 1776 AM. REVOLUTION | 1787 U.S. CONSTITUTION | 1813 | 1861 U.S. CIVIL WAR

WHERE DID JOHNNY APPLESEED WALK?

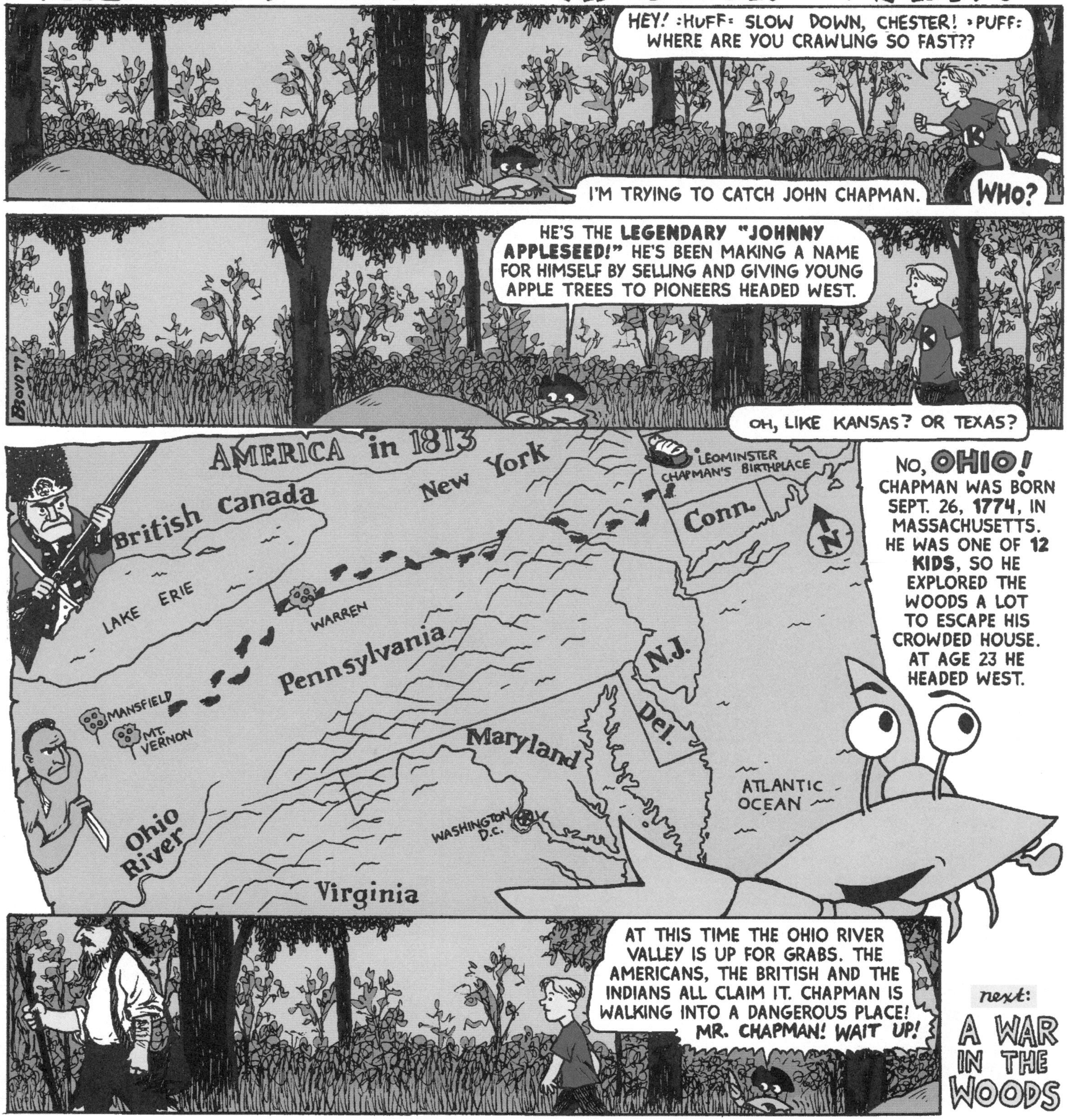

HEY! :HUFF: SLOW DOWN, CHESTER! :PUFF: WHERE ARE YOU CRAWLING SO FAST??
I'M TRYING TO CATCH JOHN CHAPMAN.
WHO?
HE'S THE LEGENDARY "JOHNNY APPLESEED!" HE'S BEEN MAKING A NAME FOR HIMSELF BY SELLING AND GIVING YOUNG APPLE TREES TO PIONEERS HEADED WEST.
OH, LIKE KANSAS? OR TEXAS?
BOYD '07
AMERICA in 1813
British canada
New York
LEOMINSTER CHAPMAN'S BIRTHPLACE
Conn.
N
LAKE ERIE
WARREN
Pennsylvania
N.J.
MANSFIELD
MT. VERNON
Del.
Maryland
ATLANTIC OCEAN
Ohio River
WASHINGTON D.C.
Virginia
NO, OHIO! CHAPMAN WAS BORN SEPT. 26, 1774, IN MASSACHUSETTS. HE WAS ONE OF 12 KIDS, SO HE EXPLORED THE WOODS A LOT TO ESCAPE HIS CROWDED HOUSE. AT AGE 23 HE HEADED WEST.
AT THIS TIME THE OHIO RIVER VALLEY IS UP FOR GRABS. THE AMERICANS, THE BRITISH AND THE INDIANS ALL CLAIM IT. CHAPMAN IS WALKING INTO A DANGEROUS PLACE!
MR. CHAPMAN! WAIT UP!
next: A WAR IN THE WOODS

CHESTER THE CRAB | 1776 AM. REVOLUTION | 1787 U.S. CONSTITUTION | 1813 | 1861 U.S. CIVIL WAR

WHEN WAS A WAR IN THE WOODS?

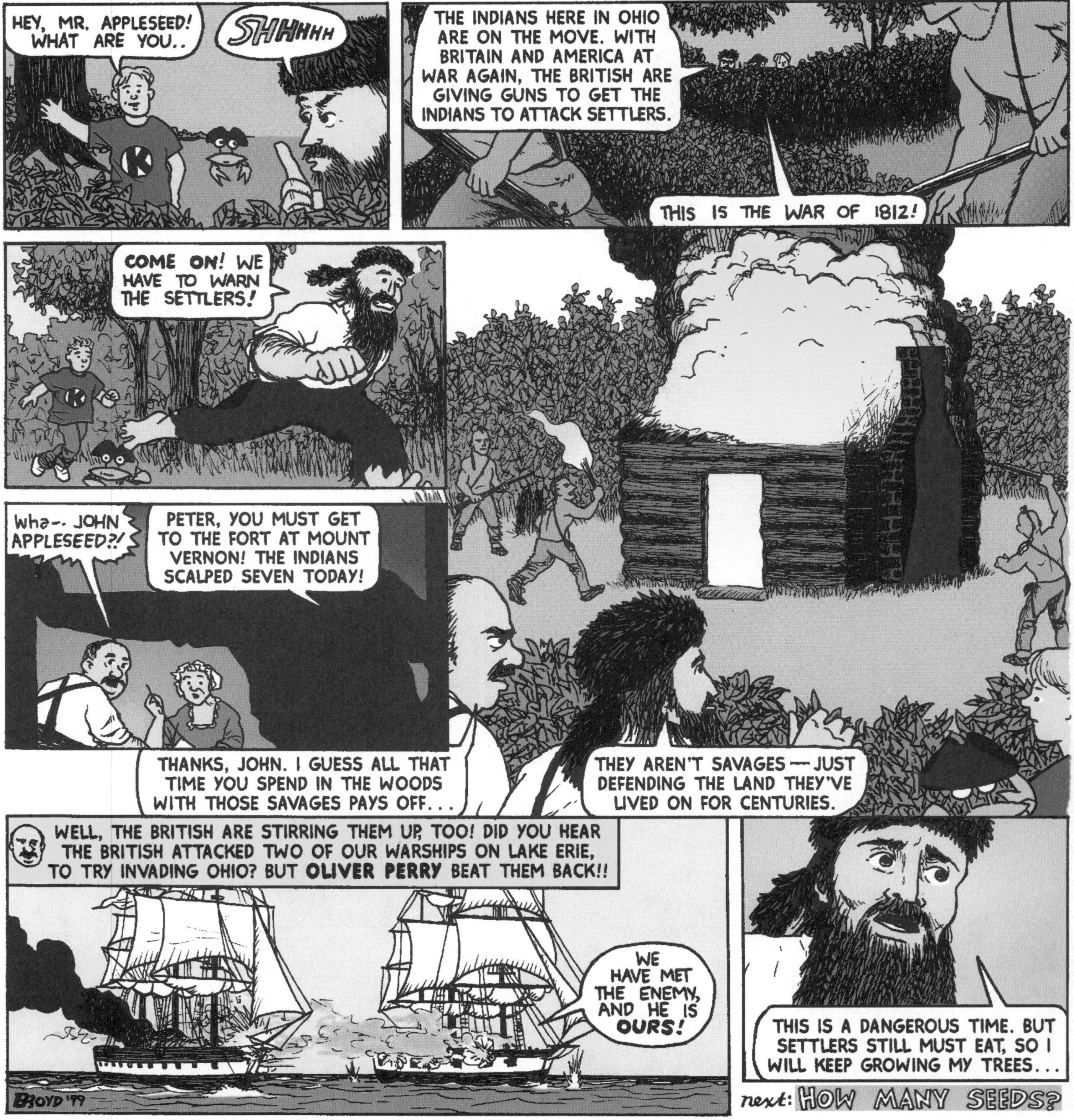

HEY, MR. APPLESEED! WHAT ARE YOU..
SHHHHHH
THE INDIANS HERE IN OHIO ARE ON THE MOVE. WITH BRITAIN AND AMERICA AT WAR AGAIN, THE BRITISH ARE GIVING GUNS TO GET THE INDIANS TO ATTACK SETTLERS.
THIS IS THE WAR OF 1812!
COME ON! WE HAVE TO WARN THE SETTLERS!
Wha-. JOHN APPLESEED?!
PETER, YOU MUST GET TO THE FORT AT MOUNT VERNON! THE INDIANS SCALPED SEVEN TODAY!
THANKS, JOHN. I GUESS ALL THAT TIME YOU SPEND IN THE WOODS WITH THOSE SAVAGES PAYS OFF...
THEY AREN'T SAVAGES — JUST DEFENDING THE LAND THEY'VE LIVED ON FOR CENTURIES.
WELL, THE BRITISH ARE STIRRING THEM UP, TOO! DID YOU HEAR THE BRITISH ATTACKED TWO OF OUR WARSHIPS ON LAKE ERIE, TO TRY INVADING OHIO? BUT OLIVER PERRY BEAT THEM BACK!!
WE HAVE MET THE ENEMY, AND HE IS OURS!
THIS IS A DANGEROUS TIME. BUT SETTLERS STILL MUST EAT, SO I WILL KEEP GROWING MY TREES...
BROYD '99
next: HOW MANY SEEDS?

HOW MANY APPLE SEEDS DID HE PLANT?

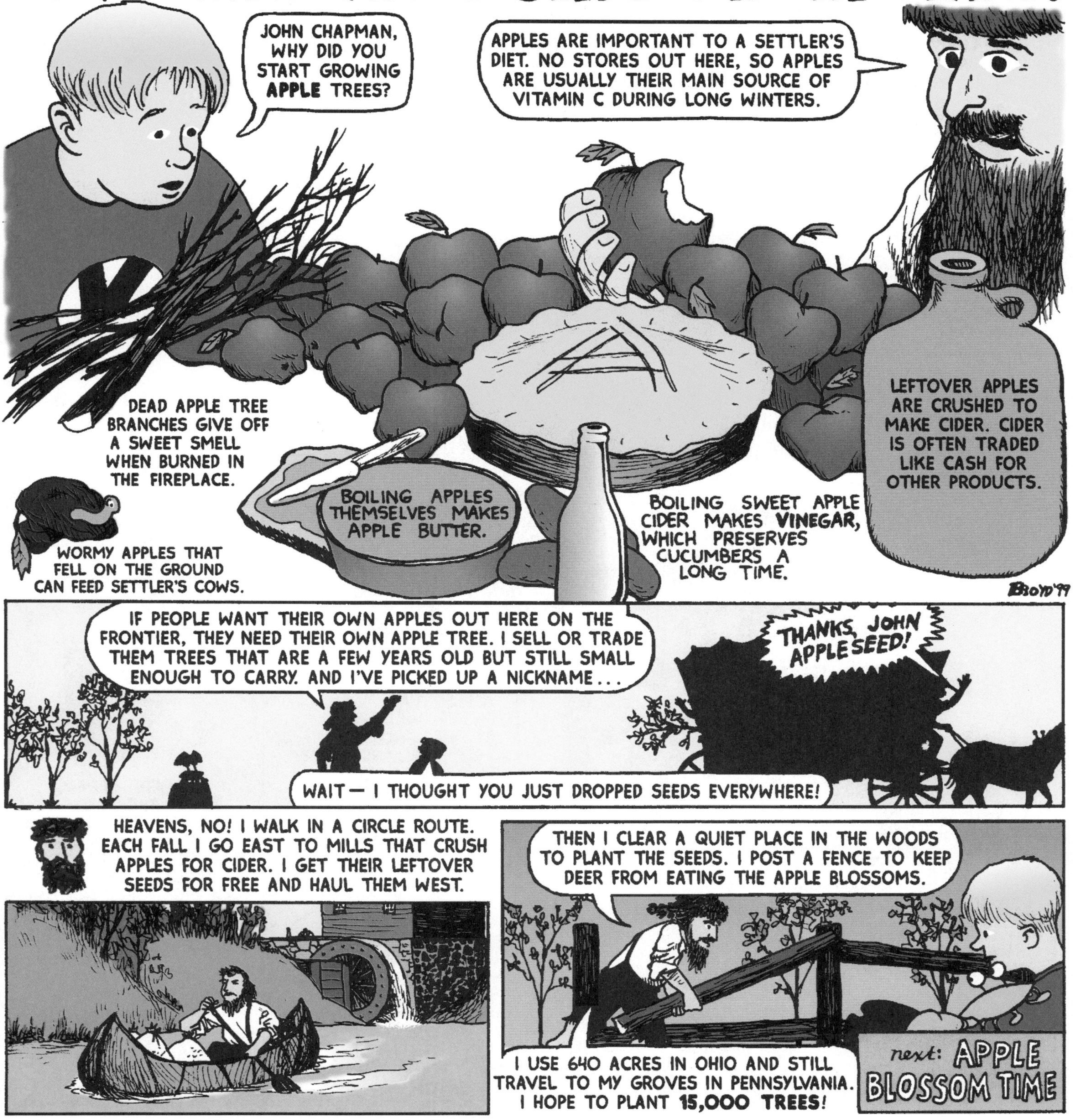
JOHN CHAPMAN, WHY DID YOU START GROWING **APPLE** TREES?
APPLES ARE IMPORTANT TO A SETTLER'S DIET. NO STORES OUT HERE, SO APPLES ARE USUALLY THEIR MAIN SOURCE OF VITAMIN C DURING LONG WINTERS.
DEAD APPLE TREE BRANCHES GIVE OFF A SWEET SMELL WHEN BURNED IN THE FIREPLACE.
WORMY APPLES THAT FELL ON THE GROUND CAN FEED SETTLER'S COWS.
BOILING APPLES THEMSELVES MAKES APPLE BUTTER.
BOILING SWEET APPLE CIDER MAKES **VINEGAR**, WHICH PRESERVES CUCUMBERS A LONG TIME.
LEFTOVER APPLES ARE CRUSHED TO MAKE CIDER. CIDER IS OFTEN TRADED LIKE CASH FOR OTHER PRODUCTS.
BOYD '99
IF PEOPLE WANT THEIR OWN APPLES OUT HERE ON THE FRONTIER, THEY NEED THEIR OWN APPLE TREE. I SELL OR TRADE THEM TREES THAT ARE A FEW YEARS OLD BUT STILL SMALL ENOUGH TO CARRY. AND I'VE PICKED UP A NICKNAME . . .
THANKS, JOHN APPLESEED!
WAIT— I THOUGHT YOU JUST DROPPED SEEDS EVERYWHERE!
HEAVENS, NO! I WALK IN A CIRCLE ROUTE. EACH FALL I GO EAST TO MILLS THAT CRUSH APPLES FOR CIDER. I GET THEIR LEFTOVER SEEDS FOR FREE AND HAUL THEM WEST.
THEN I CLEAR A QUIET PLACE IN THE WOODS TO PLANT THE SEEDS. I POST A FENCE TO KEEP DEER FROM EATING THE APPLE BLOSSOMS.
I USE 640 ACRES IN OHIO AND STILL TRAVEL TO MY GROVES IN PENNSYLVANIA. I HOPE TO PLANT **15,000 TREES**!
next: APPLE BLOSSOM TIME

HOW DO FLOWERS BECOME APPLES?

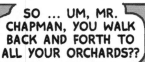

SO ... UM, MR. CHAPMAN, YOU WALK BACK AND FORTH TO ALL YOUR ORCHARDS??

YES! APPLE TREES NEED A **LOT** OF CARE TO GROW WELL. EVEN IN WINTERTIME I MUST PRUNE MY TREES – I CUT SOME BRANCES TO LET MORE SUNLIGHT IN...

IN THE SPRING THE EXTRA LIGHT HELPS BUDS GROW.

THE BUDS PRODUCE LEAVES **AND** FLOWERS. THE FLOWERS ARE APPLE BLOSSOMS.

IN LATE SPRING BEES ARE BUSY FLYING FROM BLOSSOM TO BLOSSOM TO GET NECTAR. AS THEY TRAVEL THEY SPREAD ONE BLOSSOM'S POLLEN TO ANOTHER. THAT'S CALLED **POLLINATION**. THIS POLLINATION CHANGES THE BLOSSOMS INTO APPLES!

IN THE FALL THE APPLES ARE BIG ENOUGH TO PICK.

APPLES THAT AREN'T PICKED WILL FALL TO THE GROUND. THEY ROT, AND THEIR SEEDS WILL TRY TO GROW INTO A NEW TREE.

RAIN AND SUN HELP THE APPLES GROW THROUGH THE SUMMER.

AFTER POLLINATION, THE PETALS OF THE BLOSSOM FALL OFF, LEAVING THE TINY APPLE AT THE CENTER OF THE LEAVES.

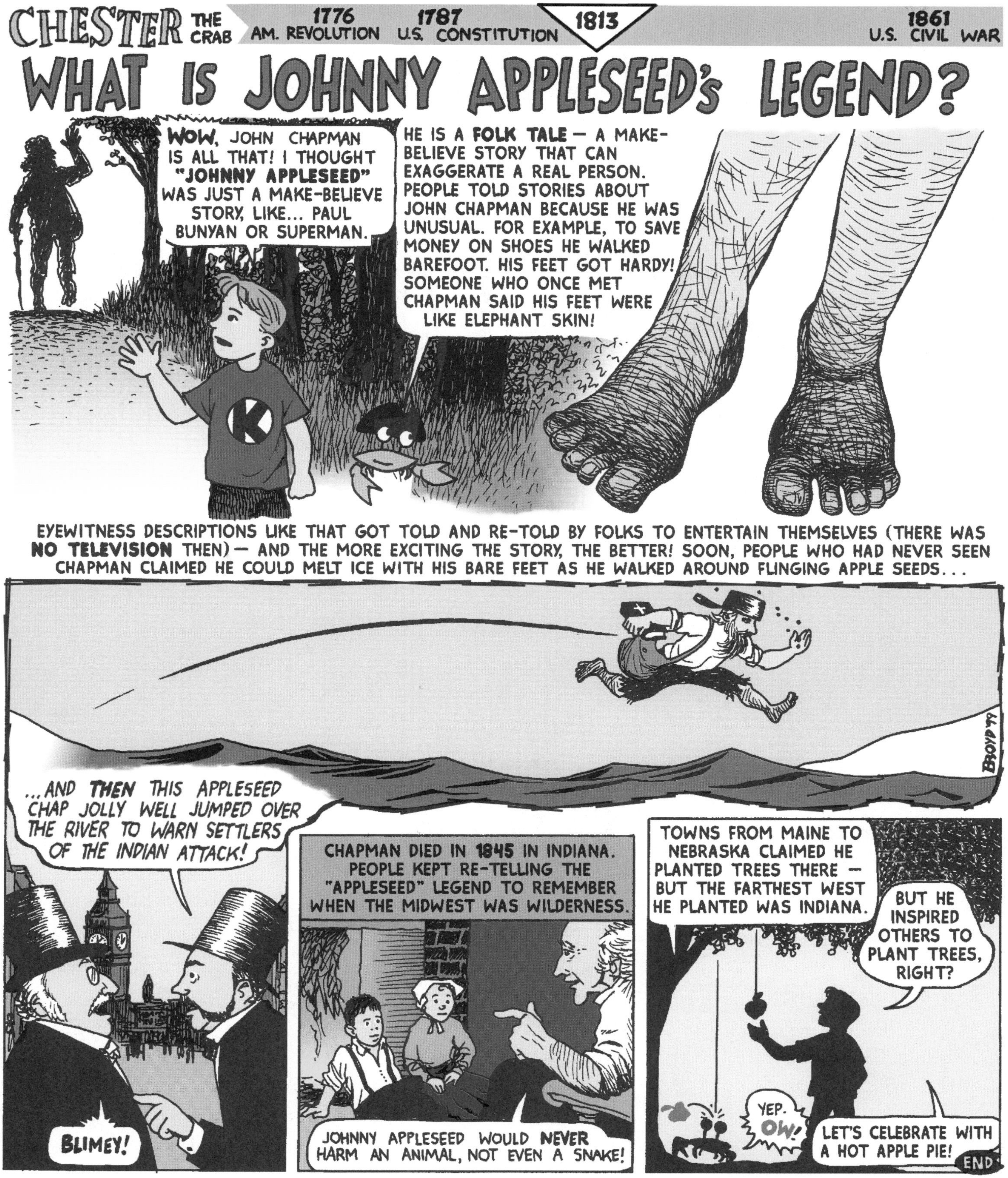
CHESTER THE CRAB
1776 AM. REVOLUTION
1787 U.S. CONSTITUTION
1813
1861 U.S. CIVIL WAR
WHAT IS JOHNNY APPLESEED's LEGEND?
WOW, JOHN CHAPMAN IS ALL THAT! I THOUGHT "JOHNNY APPLESEED" WAS JUST A MAKE-BELIEVE STORY, LIKE... PAUL BUNYAN OR SUPERMAN.
HE IS A FOLK TALE — A MAKE-BELIEVE STORY THAT CAN EXAGGERATE A REAL PERSON. PEOPLE TOLD STORIES ABOUT JOHN CHAPMAN BECAUSE HE WAS UNUSUAL. FOR EXAMPLE, TO SAVE MONEY ON SHOES HE WALKED BAREFOOT. HIS FEET GOT HARDY! SOMEONE WHO ONCE MET CHAPMAN SAID HIS FEET WERE LIKE ELEPHANT SKIN!
EYEWITNESS DESCRIPTIONS LIKE THAT GOT TOLD AND RE-TOLD BY FOLKS TO ENTERTAIN THEMSELVES (THERE WAS NO TELEVISION THEN) — AND THE MORE EXCITING THE STORY, THE BETTER! SOON, PEOPLE WHO HAD NEVER SEEN CHAPMAN CLAIMED HE COULD MELT ICE WITH HIS BARE FEET AS HE WALKED AROUND FLINGING APPLE SEEDS...
BROYD '99
...AND THEN THIS APPLESEED CHAP JOLLY WELL JUMPED OVER THE RIVER TO WARN SETTLERS OF THE INDIAN ATTACK!
BLIMEY!
CHAPMAN DIED IN 1845 IN INDIANA. PEOPLE KEPT RE-TELLING THE "APPLESEED" LEGEND TO REMEMBER WHEN THE MIDWEST WAS WILDERNESS.
JOHNNY APPLESEED WOULD NEVER HARM AN ANIMAL, NOT EVEN A SNAKE!
TOWNS FROM MAINE TO NEBRASKA CLAIMED HE PLANTED TREES THERE — BUT THE FARTHEST WEST HE PLANTED WAS INDIANA.
BUT HE INSPIRED OTHERS TO PLANT TREES, RIGHT?
YEP. OW!
LET'S CELEBRATE WITH A HOT APPLE PIE!
END

CHAPTER 2

DAVY CROCKETT

Frontiersman Davy Crockett's legend was so popular in the 1950s that American boys begged for fake coonskin caps to wear on their imaginary adventures. But Davy was a real man of the early 1800s who also served in Congress and defended the rights of American Indians. His own legend got a publicity boost when people started a campaign to make him president of the United States . . .

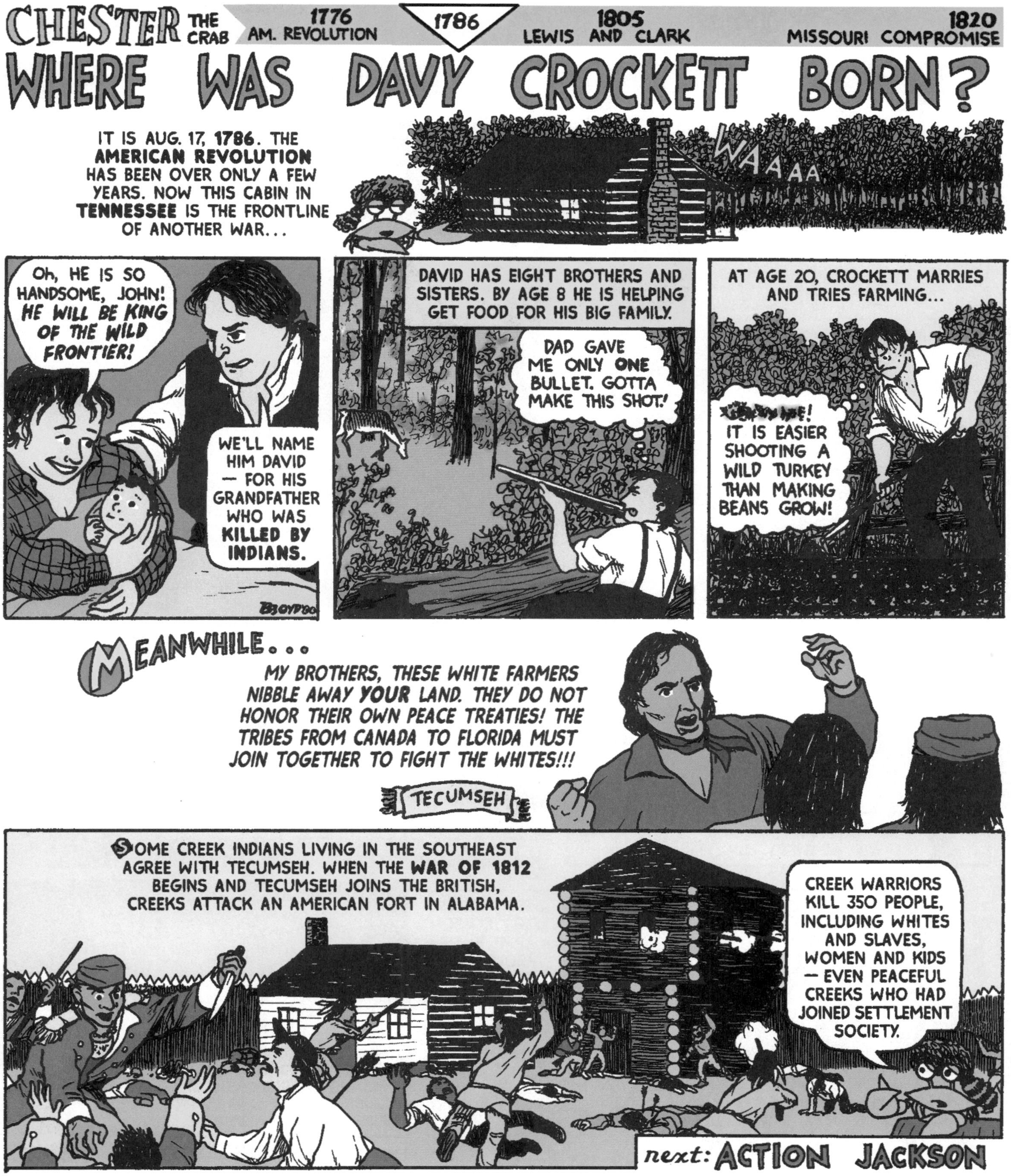
CHESTER THE CRAB
1776 AM. REVOLUTION
1786
1805 LEWIS AND CLARK
1820 MISSOURI COMPROMISE
WHERE WAS DAVY CROCKETT BORN?
IT IS AUG. 17, 1786. THE AMERICAN REVOLUTION HAS BEEN OVER ONLY A FEW YEARS. NOW THIS CABIN IN TENNESSEE IS THE FRONTLINE OF ANOTHER WAR...
WAAAAA
Oh, HE IS SO HANDSOME, JOHN! HE WILL BE KING OF THE WILD FRONTIER!
WE'LL NAME HIM DAVID — FOR HIS GRANDFATHER WHO WAS KILLED BY INDIANS.
BOYD'00
DAVID HAS EIGHT BROTHERS AND SISTERS. BY AGE 8 HE IS HELPING GET FOOD FOR HIS BIG FAMILY.
DAD GAVE ME ONLY ONE BULLET. GOTTA MAKE THIS SHOT!
AT AGE 20, CROCKETT MARRIES AND TRIES FARMING...
! IT IS EASIER SHOOTING A WILD TURKEY THAN MAKING BEANS GROW!
MEANWHILE...
MY BROTHERS, THESE WHITE FARMERS NIBBLE AWAY YOUR LAND. THEY DO NOT HONOR THEIR OWN PEACE TREATIES! THE TRIBES FROM CANADA TO FLORIDA MUST JOIN TOGETHER TO FIGHT THE WHITES!!!
TECUMSEH
SOME CREEK INDIANS LIVING IN THE SOUTHEAST AGREE WITH TECUMSEH. WHEN THE WAR OF 1812 BEGINS AND TECUMSEH JOINS THE BRITISH, CREEKS ATTACK AN AMERICAN FORT IN ALABAMA.
CREEK WARRIORS KILL 350 PEOPLE, INCLUDING WHITES AND SLAVES, WOMEN AND KIDS — EVEN PEACEFUL CREEKS WHO HAD JOINED SETTLEMENT SOCIETY.
next: ACTION JACKSON

CHESTER THE CRAB 1776 AM. REVOLUTION 1787 U.S. CONSTITUTION 1813 1820 MISSOURI COMPROMISE

WHO FOUGHT CREEK INDIANS IN 1813?

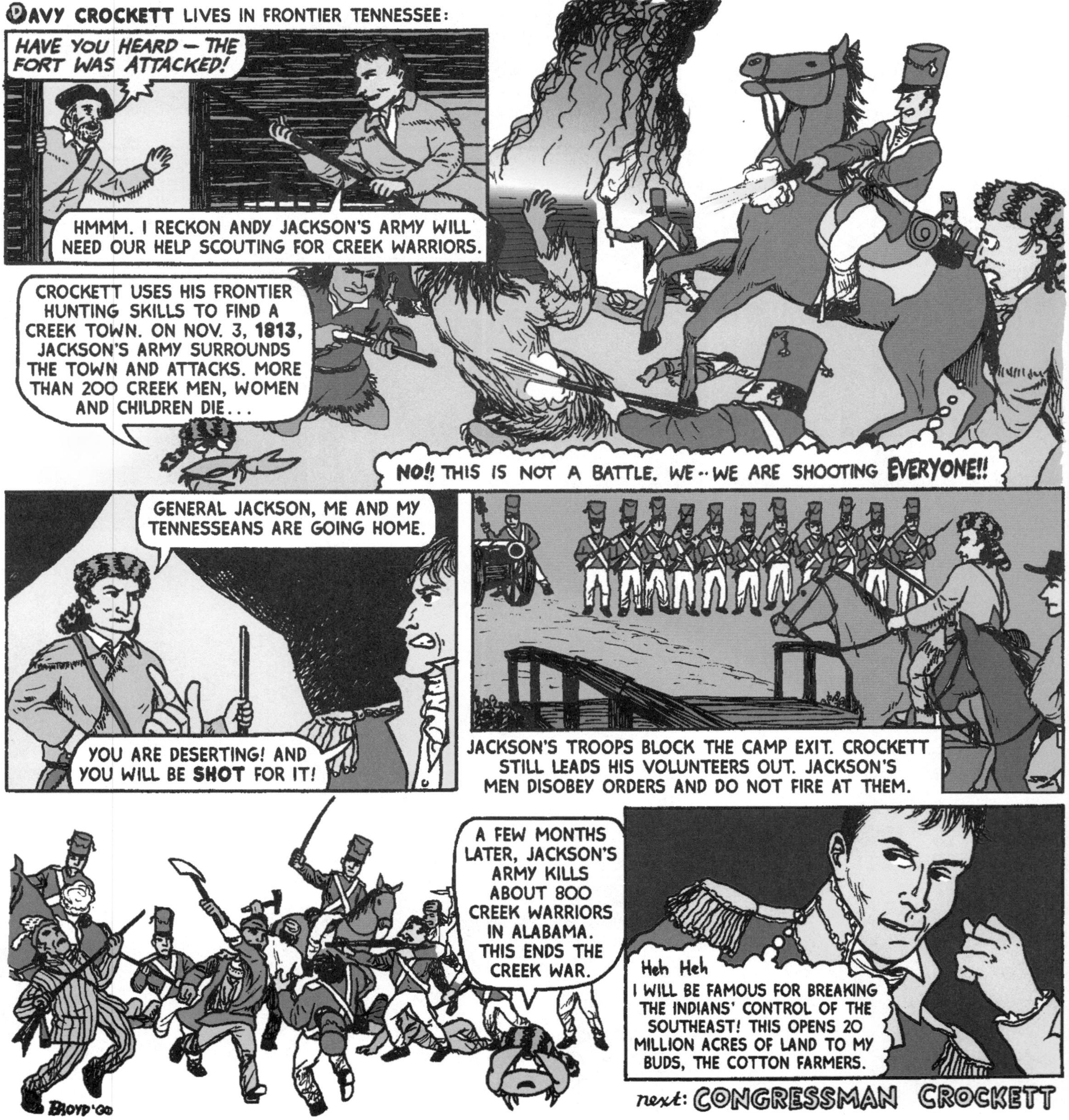

DAVY CROCKETT LIVES IN FRONTIER TENNESSEE:
HAVE YOU HEARD — THE FORT WAS ATTACKED!
HMMM. I RECKON ANDY JACKSON'S ARMY WILL NEED OUR HELP SCOUTING FOR CREEK WARRIORS.
CROCKETT USES HIS FRONTIER HUNTING SKILLS TO FIND A CREEK TOWN. ON NOV. 3, 1813, JACKSON'S ARMY SURROUNDS THE TOWN AND ATTACKS. MORE THAN 200 CREEK MEN, WOMEN AND CHILDREN DIE...
NO!! THIS IS NOT A BATTLE. WE -- WE ARE SHOOTING EVERYONE!!
GENERAL JACKSON, ME AND MY TENNESSEANS ARE GOING HOME.
YOU ARE DESERTING! AND YOU WILL BE SHOT FOR IT!
JACKSON'S TROOPS BLOCK THE CAMP EXIT. CROCKETT STILL LEADS HIS VOLUNTEERS OUT. JACKSON'S MEN DISOBEY ORDERS AND DO NOT FIRE AT THEM.
A FEW MONTHS LATER, JACKSON'S ARMY KILLS ABOUT 800 CREEK WARRIORS IN ALABAMA. THIS ENDS THE CREEK WAR.
Heh Heh
I WILL BE FAMOUS FOR BREAKING THE INDIANS' CONTROL OF THE SOUTHEAST! THIS OPENS 20 MILLION ACRES OF LAND TO MY BUDS, THE COTTON FARMERS.
BLOYD '00
next: CONGRESSMAN CROCKETT

WHO FOUGHT ANDREW JACKSON IN D.C.?

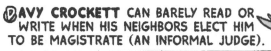

DAVY CROCKETT CAN BARELY READ OR WRITE WHEN HIS NEIGHBORS ELECT HIM TO BE MAGISTRATE (AN INFORMAL JUDGE).

EVERYONE WHO CAME TO MY BARBEQUE BROUGHT FOOD. TOM HERE GAVE ME A PIG.

THEN HE SERVED US BARBEQUED **RACCOON!**

Heh! JOE, YOU OWE TOM A PIG. IT IS COMMON SENSE.

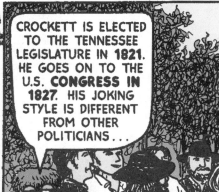

CROCKETT IS ELECTED TO THE TENNESSEE LEGISLATURE IN **1821**. HE GOES ON TO THE U.S. **CONGRESS IN 1827**. HIS JOKING STYLE IS DIFFERENT FROM OTHER POLITICIANS . . .

CIDER

I AM **DAVY CROCKETT** — HALF HORSE, HALF ALLIGATOR, WITH A TOUCH OF SNAPPIN' TURTLE!! COME HAVE A DRINK!

IN CONGRESS HE FIGHTS FOR SQUATTERS' RIGHTS. HE SAYS PEOPLE MAKING FARMS ON THE FRONTIER SHOULD GET TO BUY THAT LAND CHEAP.

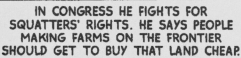

THESE FARMERS ARE THE **TRUE** AMERICANS — NOT THOSE SLAVE-OWNING PLANTERS WHO CONTROL PRESIDENT JACKSON!!

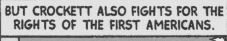

BUT CROCKETT ALSO FIGHTS FOR THE RIGHTS OF THE FIRST AMERICANS.

MISSISSIPPI R.

UNITED STATES

GULF OF MEXICO

JACKSON WANTS TO SEND **ALL** INDIANS WEST OF THE MISSISSIPPI RIVER. THIS BREAKS OUR TREATIES WITH THEM!! CAN'T WE LIVE SIDE-BY-SIDE?

A.J.

THIS BACKWOODS HICK IS EMBARRASSING ME! **GET RID OF CROCKETT!**

A NEW POLITICAL PARTY — THE **WHIGS** — SENDS CROCKETT ON A NATIONAL TOUR. THEY HOPE TO MAKE HIM POPULAR ENOUGH TO WIN THE PRESIDENCY.

THE TOUR **DOES** PUMP UP CROCKETT'S LEGEND. BUT JACKSON'S MEN KILL CROCKETT'S BILLS IN CONGRESS. IN 1835 THEY ALSO PUSH HIM OUT OF OFFICE.

YOU CAN ALL GO TO BLAZES! I'M GOING TO TEXAS!

next!

WHY DO WE REMEMBER THE ALAMO?

DAVY CROCKETT SHOWS UP IN SAN ANTONIO, **TEXAS**, IN JANUARY **1836**...

WILLIAM TRAVIS, I AM HERE TO HELP Y 'ALL FIGHT FOR YOUR INDEPENDENCE FROM MEXICO.

MEXICAN PRESIDENT-GENERAL ANTONIO LOPEZ DE SANTA ANNA SAYS THESE AMERICANS ARE INVADERS OF MEXICAN LAND. IN FEBRUARY HIS ARMY SURROUNDS TRAVIS AND HIS MEN IN **THE ALAMO**.

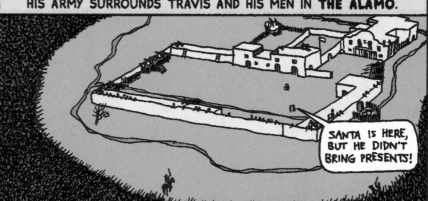

SANTA IS HERE, BUT HE DIDN'T BRING PRESENTS!

FOR 13 DAYS, ABOUT 185 MEN HOLD OFF THE 5,000 MEXICAN SOLDIERS. ON MARCH 6, THE MEXICAN ARMY FINALLY OVERRUNS CROCKETT AND COMPANY IN THE OLD SPANISH CHURCH.

SOME WOMEN AND A SLAVE SURVIVE IN THE ALAMO. CROCKETT DOESN'T.

HOUSTON, WE HAVE A PROBLEM!

SANTA ANNA MOVES EAST TO ATTACK AMERICANS LED BY **SAM HOUSTON**. HOUSTON DEFEATS THE MEXICAN ARMY NEAR THE SAN JACINTO RIVER.

REMEMBER THE ALAMO!!

TEXAS BECOMES A REPUBLIC — ITS OWN COUNTRY! HOUSTON IS ITS PRESIDENT. THE UNITED STATES ANNEXES TEXAS AS THE 28TH STATE IN **1845**. END

BROYD '00

CHAPTER 3

SAM HOUSTON

He was called **"The Raven"** when he lived with the Cherokee Indians. **Sam Houston** was a hero similar to Davy Crockett - always on the move between the American settlements and the Native American towns on the frontier. And when the frontier moved west and hit Texas, both Crockett and Houston would find their destiny there . . .

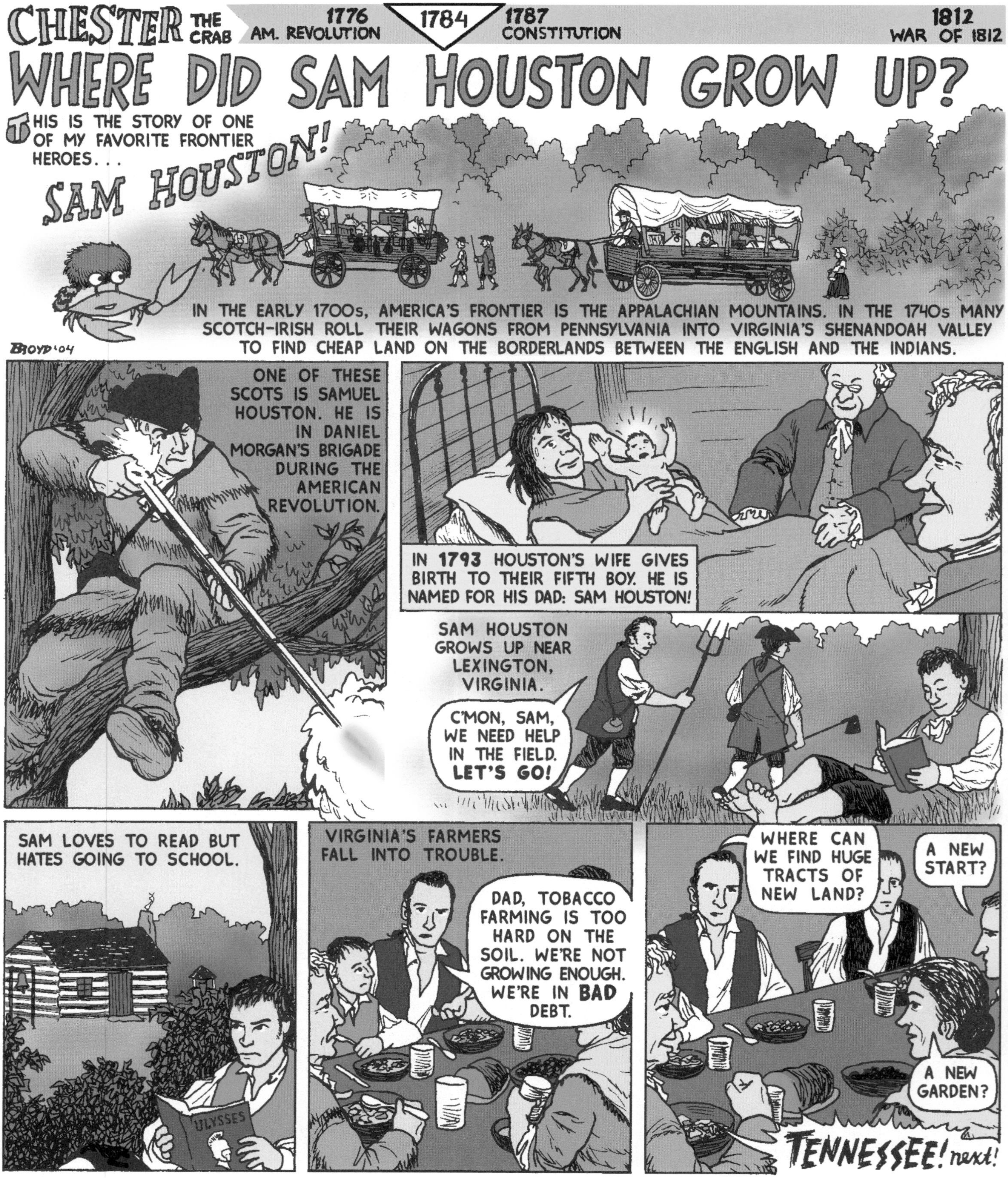

CHESTER THE CRAB
1776 AM. REVOLUTION
1784
1787 CONSTITUTION
1812 WAR OF 1812
WHERE DID SAM HOUSTON GROW UP?
THIS IS THE STORY OF ONE OF MY FAVORITE FRONTIER HEROES. . .
SAM HOUSTON!
IN THE EARLY 1700s, AMERICA'S FRONTIER IS THE APPALACHIAN MOUNTAINS. IN THE 1740s MANY SCOTCH-IRISH ROLL THEIR WAGONS FROM PENNSYLVANIA INTO VIRGINIA'S SHENANDOAH VALLEY TO FIND CHEAP LAND ON THE BORDERLANDS BETWEEN THE ENGLISH AND THE INDIANS.
BROYD '04
ONE OF THESE SCOTS IS SAMUEL HOUSTON. HE IS IN DANIEL MORGAN'S BRIGADE DURING THE AMERICAN REVOLUTION.
IN 1793 HOUSTON'S WIFE GIVES BIRTH TO THEIR FIFTH BOY. HE IS NAMED FOR HIS DAD: SAM HOUSTON!
SAM HOUSTON GROWS UP NEAR LEXINGTON, VIRGINIA.
C'MON, SAM, WE NEED HELP IN THE FIELD. LET'S GO!
SAM LOVES TO READ BUT HATES GOING TO SCHOOL.
ULYSSES
VIRGINIA'S FARMERS FALL INTO TROUBLE.
DAD, TOBACCO FARMING IS TOO HARD ON THE SOIL. WE'RE NOT GROWING ENOUGH. WE'RE IN BAD DEBT.
WHERE CAN WE FIND HUGE TRACTS OF NEW LAND?
A NEW START?
A NEW GARDEN?
TENNESSEE! next!

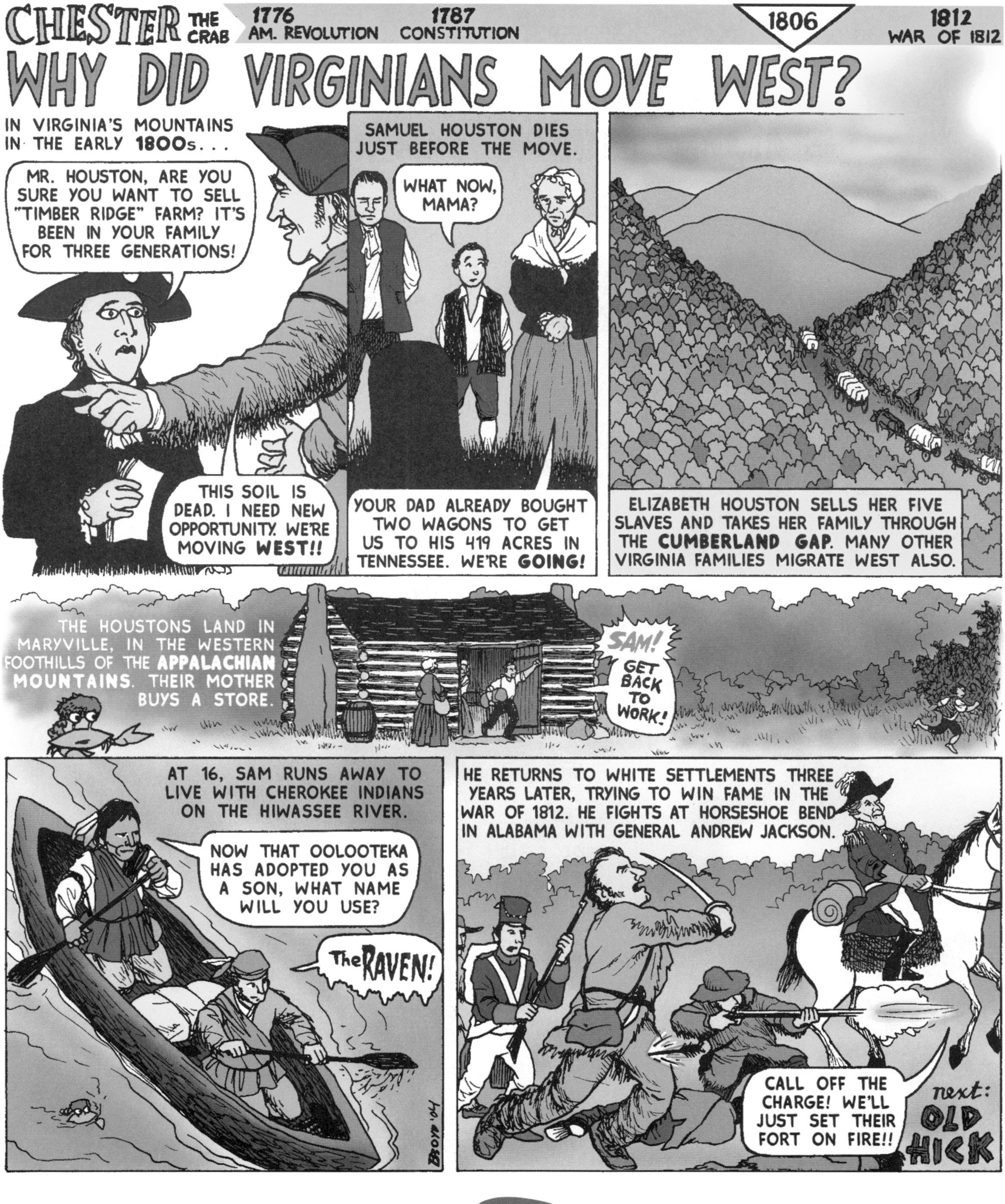

CHESTER THE CRAB
1776 AM. REVOLUTION
1787 CONSTITUTION
1806
1812 WAR OF 1812
WHY DID VIRGINIANS MOVE WEST?
IN VIRGINIA'S MOUNTAINS IN THE EARLY 1800s...
MR. HOUSTON, ARE YOU SURE YOU WANT TO SELL "TIMBER RIDGE" FARM? IT'S BEEN IN YOUR FAMILY FOR THREE GENERATIONS!
THIS SOIL IS DEAD. I NEED NEW OPPORTUNITY. WE'RE MOVING WEST!!
SAMUEL HOUSTON DIES JUST BEFORE THE MOVE.
WHAT NOW, MAMA?
YOUR DAD ALREADY BOUGHT TWO WAGONS TO GET US TO HIS 419 ACRES IN TENNESSEE. WE'RE GOING!
ELIZABETH HOUSTON SELLS HER FIVE SLAVES AND TAKES HER FAMILY THROUGH THE CUMBERLAND GAP. MANY OTHER VIRGINIA FAMILIES MIGRATE WEST ALSO.
THE HOUSTONS LAND IN MARYVILLE, IN THE WESTERN FOOTHILLS OF THE APPALACHIAN MOUNTAINS. THEIR MOTHER BUYS A STORE.
SAM! GET BACK TO WORK!
AT 16, SAM RUNS AWAY TO LIVE WITH CHEROKEE INDIANS ON THE HIWASSEE RIVER.
NOW THAT OOLOOTEKA HAS ADOPTED YOU AS A SON, WHAT NAME WILL YOU USE?
The RAVEN!
BBOYD '04
HE RETURNS TO WHITE SETTLEMENTS THREE YEARS LATER, TRYING TO WIN FAME IN THE WAR OF 1812. HE FIGHTS AT HORSESHOE BEND IN ALABAMA WITH GENERAL ANDREW JACKSON.
CALL OFF THE CHARGE! WE'LL JUST SET THEIR FORT ON FIRE!!
next: OLD HICK

HOW DID JACKSON & HOUSTON DIFFER?

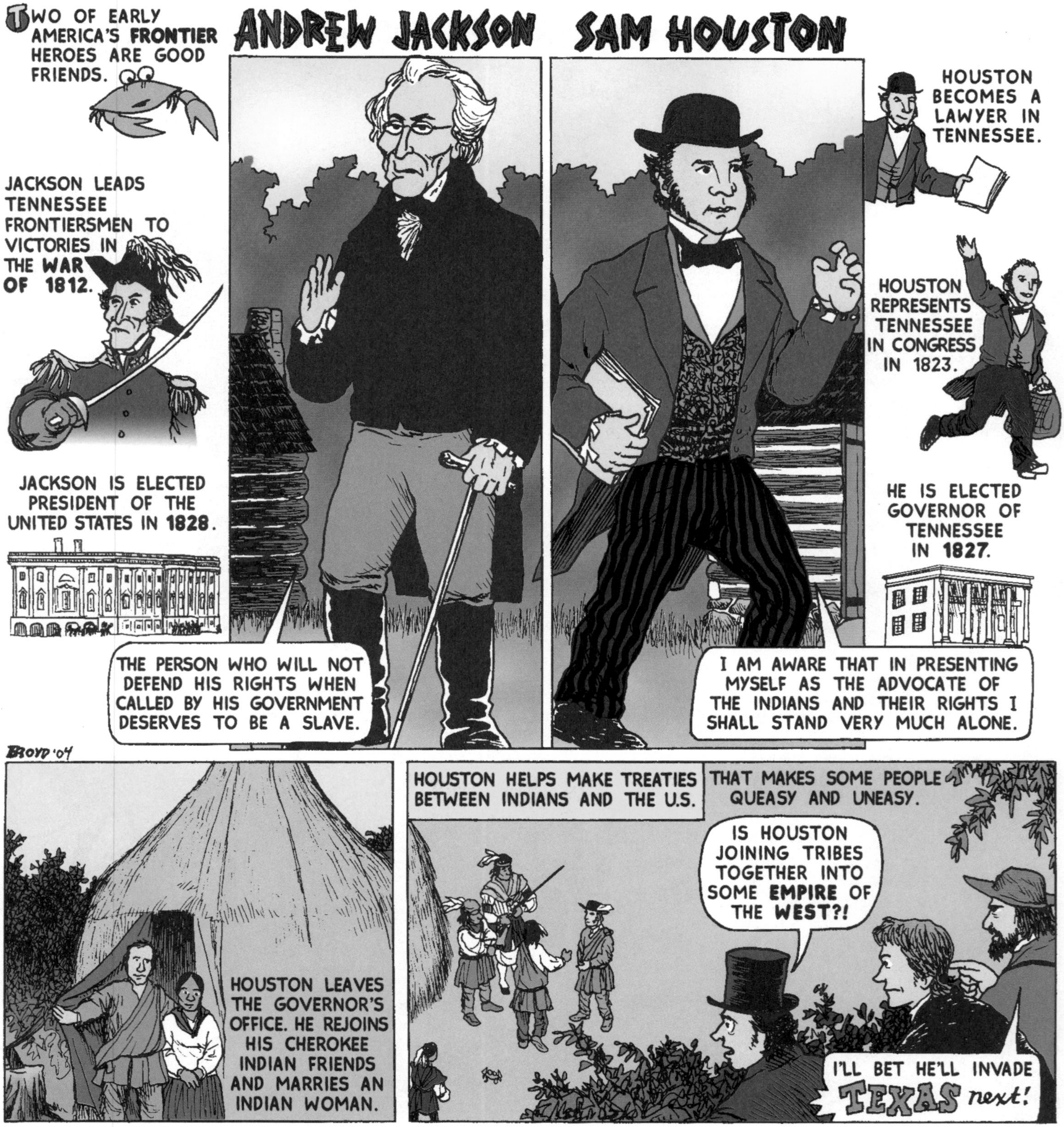
TWO OF EARLY AMERICA'S FRONTIER HEROES ARE GOOD FRIENDS.
ANDREW JACKSON
SAM HOUSTON
JACKSON LEADS TENNESSEE FRONTIERSMEN TO VICTORIES IN THE WAR OF 1812.
JACKSON IS ELECTED PRESIDENT OF THE UNITED STATES IN 1828.
THE PERSON WHO WILL NOT DEFEND HIS RIGHTS WHEN CALLED BY HIS GOVERNMENT DESERVES TO BE A SLAVE.
HOUSTON BECOMES A LAWYER IN TENNESSEE.
HOUSTON REPRESENTS TENNESSEE IN CONGRESS IN 1823.
HE IS ELECTED GOVERNOR OF TENNESSEE IN 1827.
I AM AWARE THAT IN PRESENTING MYSELF AS THE ADVOCATE OF THE INDIANS AND THEIR RIGHTS I SHALL STAND VERY MUCH ALONE.
HOUSTON LEAVES THE GOVERNOR'S OFFICE. HE REJOINS HIS CHEROKEE INDIAN FRIENDS AND MARRIES AN INDIAN WOMAN.
HOUSTON HELPS MAKE TREATIES BETWEEN INDIANS AND THE U.S.
THAT MAKES SOME PEOPLE QUEASY AND UNEASY.
IS HOUSTON JOINING TRIBES TOGETHER INTO SOME EMPIRE OF THE WEST?!
I'LL BET HE'LL INVADE TEXAS next!

HOW DOES HOUSTON LEAD THE TEXANS?

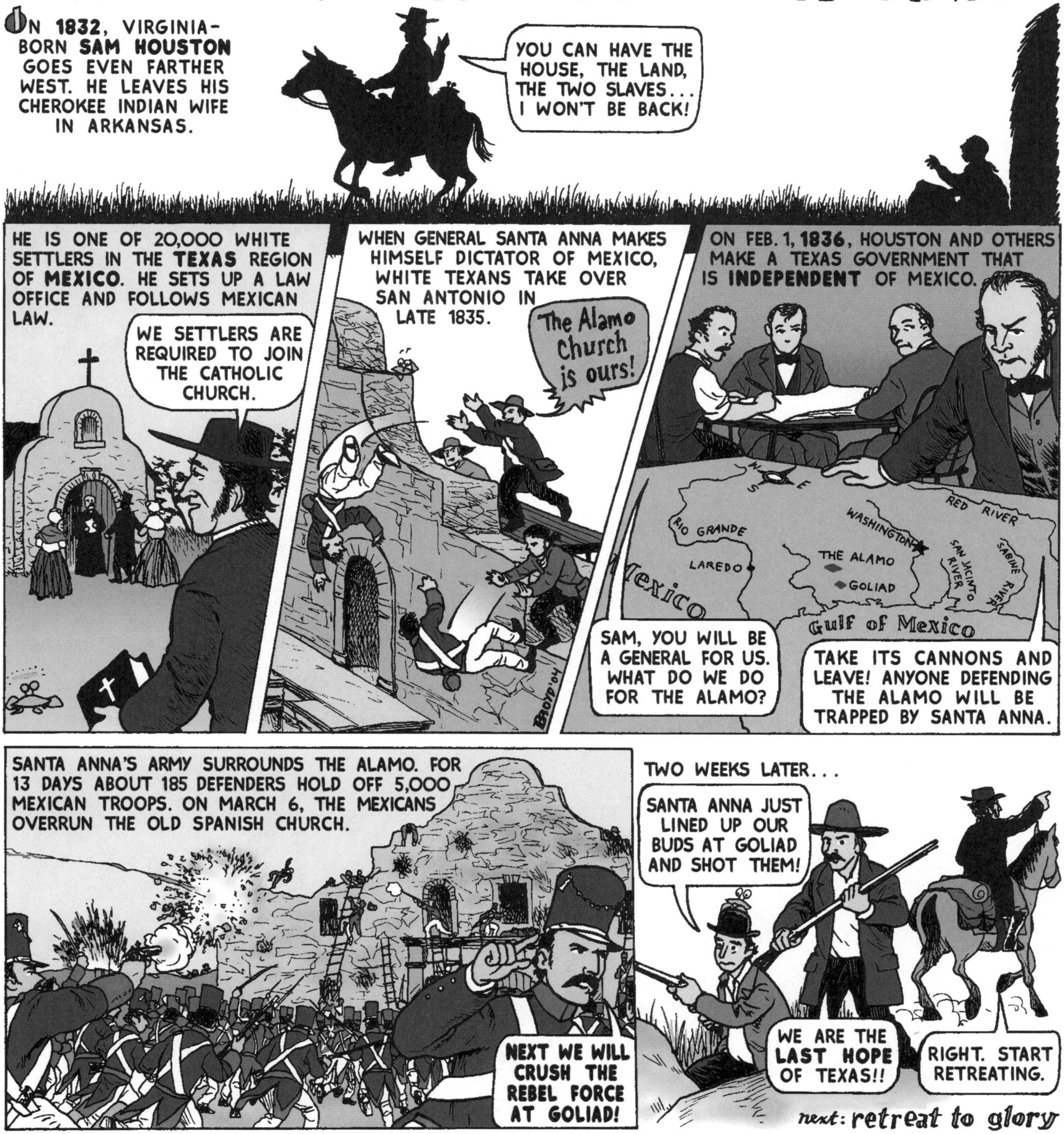
IN 1832, VIRGINIA-BORN SAM HOUSTON GOES EVEN FARTHER WEST. HE LEAVES HIS CHEROKEE INDIAN WIFE IN ARKANSAS.
YOU CAN HAVE THE HOUSE, THE LAND, THE TWO SLAVES... I WON'T BE BACK!
HE IS ONE OF 20,000 WHITE SETTLERS IN THE TEXAS REGION OF MEXICO. HE SETS UP A LAW OFFICE AND FOLLOWS MEXICAN LAW.
WE SETTLERS ARE REQUIRED TO JOIN THE CATHOLIC CHURCH.
WHEN GENERAL SANTA ANNA MAKES HIMSELF DICTATOR OF MEXICO, WHITE TEXANS TAKE OVER SAN ANTONIO IN LATE 1835.
The Alamo Church is ours!
BROYD '04
ON FEB. 1, 1836, HOUSTON AND OTHERS MAKE A TEXAS GOVERNMENT THAT IS INDEPENDENT OF MEXICO.
RED RIVER
WASHINGTON
RIO GRANDE
LAREDO
THE ALAMO
GOLIAD
SAN JACINTO RIVER
SABINE RIVER
Mexico
Gulf of Mexico
SAM, YOU WILL BE A GENERAL FOR US. WHAT DO WE DO FOR THE ALAMO?
TAKE ITS CANNONS AND LEAVE! ANYONE DEFENDING THE ALAMO WILL BE TRAPPED BY SANTA ANNA.
SANTA ANNA'S ARMY SURROUNDS THE ALAMO. FOR 13 DAYS ABOUT 185 DEFENDERS HOLD OFF 5,000 MEXICAN TROOPS. ON MARCH 6, THE MEXICANS OVERRUN THE OLD SPANISH CHURCH.
NEXT WE WILL CRUSH THE REBEL FORCE AT GOLIAD!
TWO WEEKS LATER...
SANTA ANNA JUST LINED UP OUR BUDS AT GOLIAD AND SHOT THEM!
WE ARE THE LAST HOPE OF TEXAS!!
RIGHT. START RETREATING.

next: retreat to glory

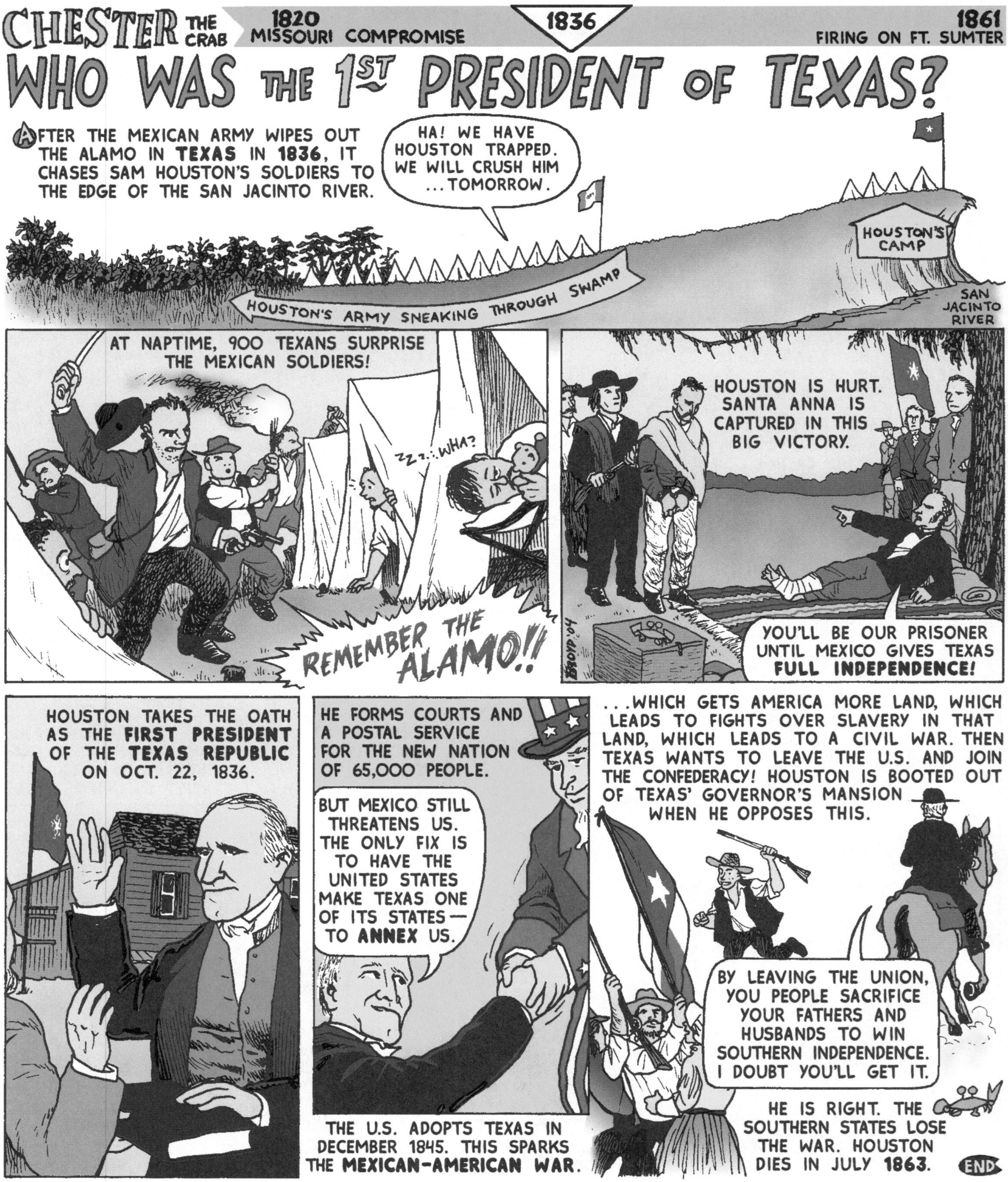
CHESTER THE CRAB
1820 MISSOURI COMPROMISE
1836
1861 FIRING ON FT. SUMTER
WHO WAS THE 1ST PRESIDENT OF TEXAS?
AFTER THE MEXICAN ARMY WIPES OUT THE ALAMO IN TEXAS IN 1836, IT CHASES SAM HOUSTON'S SOLDIERS TO THE EDGE OF THE SAN JACINTO RIVER.
HA! WE HAVE HOUSTON TRAPPED. WE WILL CRUSH HIM ...TOMORROW.
HOUSTON'S CAMP
HOUSTON'S ARMY SNEAKING THROUGH SWAMP
SAN JACINTO RIVER
AT NAPTIME, 900 TEXANS SURPRISE THE MEXICAN SOLDIERS!
Z z ... WHA?
REMEMBER THE ALAMO!!
BROYD '04
HOUSTON IS HURT. SANTA ANNA IS CAPTURED IN THIS BIG VICTORY.
YOU'LL BE OUR PRISONER UNTIL MEXICO GIVES TEXAS FULL INDEPENDENCE!
HOUSTON TAKES THE OATH AS THE FIRST PRESIDENT OF THE TEXAS REPUBLIC ON OCT. 22, 1836.
HE FORMS COURTS AND A POSTAL SERVICE FOR THE NEW NATION OF 65,000 PEOPLE.
BUT MEXICO STILL THREATENS US. THE ONLY FIX IS TO HAVE THE UNITED STATES MAKE TEXAS ONE OF ITS STATES— TO ANNEX US.
THE U.S. ADOPTS TEXAS IN DECEMBER 1845. THIS SPARKS THE MEXICAN-AMERICAN WAR.
...WHICH GETS AMERICA MORE LAND, WHICH LEADS TO FIGHTS OVER SLAVERY IN THAT LAND, WHICH LEADS TO A CIVIL WAR. THEN TEXAS WANTS TO LEAVE THE U.S. AND JOIN THE CONFEDERACY! HOUSTON IS BOOTED OUT OF TEXAS' GOVERNOR'S MANSION WHEN HE OPPOSES THIS.
BY LEAVING THE UNION, YOU PEOPLE SACRIFICE YOUR FATHERS AND HUSBANDS TO WIN SOUTHERN INDEPENDENCE. I DOUBT YOU'LL GET IT.
HE IS RIGHT. THE SOUTHERN STATES LOSE THE WAR. HOUSTON DIES IN JULY 1863.
END

JOHN HENRY

Dozens of songs, cartoons, and retellings of **railroad man John Henry** have made him seem like the most fanciful of the early American **legends**. But new research has added a lot of historical detail to his tale. John Henry is the perfect character for examining how storytelling and history connect . . .

CHESTER THE CRAB
WAS JOHN HENRY A LEGEND?

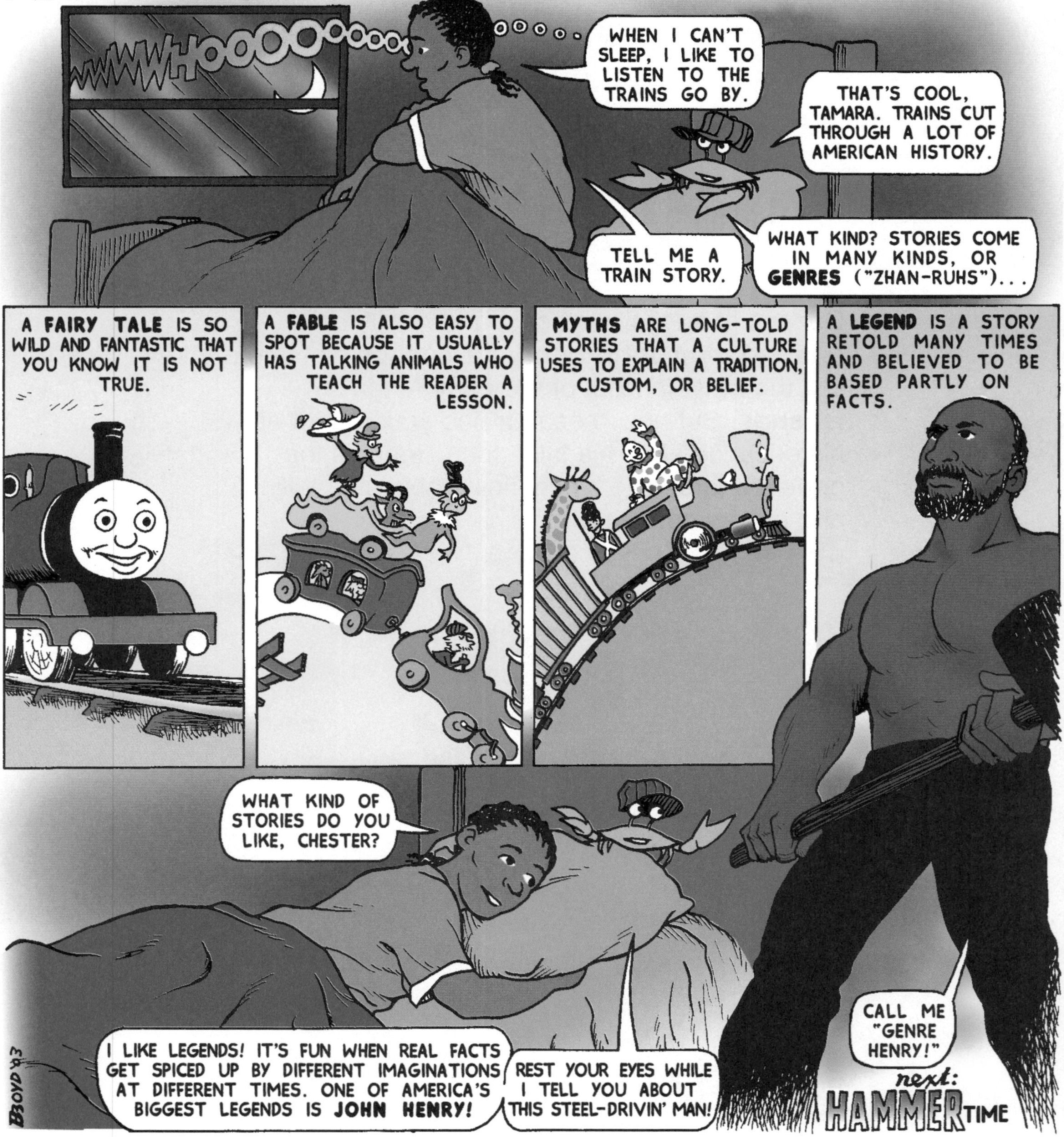

WWWWHOOOOOOOOOOooooo . . .
WHEN I CAN'T SLEEP, I LIKE TO LISTEN TO THE TRAINS GO BY.
THAT'S COOL, TAMARA. TRAINS CUT THROUGH A LOT OF AMERICAN HISTORY.
TELL ME A TRAIN STORY.
WHAT KIND? STORIES COME IN MANY KINDS, OR GENRES ("ZHAN-RUHS"). . .
A FAIRY TALE IS SO WILD AND FANTASTIC THAT YOU KNOW IT IS NOT TRUE.
A FABLE IS ALSO EASY TO SPOT BECAUSE IT USUALLY HAS TALKING ANIMALS WHO TEACH THE READER A LESSON.
MYTHS ARE LONG-TOLD STORIES THAT A CULTURE USES TO EXPLAIN A TRADITION, CUSTOM, OR BELIEF.
A LEGEND IS A STORY RETOLD MANY TIMES AND BELIEVED TO BE BASED PARTLY ON FACTS.
WHAT KIND OF STORIES DO YOU LIKE, CHESTER?
I LIKE LEGENDS! IT'S FUN WHEN REAL FACTS GET SPICED UP BY DIFFERENT IMAGINATIONS AT DIFFERENT TIMES. ONE OF AMERICA'S BIGGEST LEGENDS IS JOHN HENRY!
REST YOUR EYES WHILE I TELL YOU ABOUT THIS STEEL-DRIVIN' MAN!
CALL ME "GENRE HENRY!"
BBOYD '03

next: HAMMER TIME

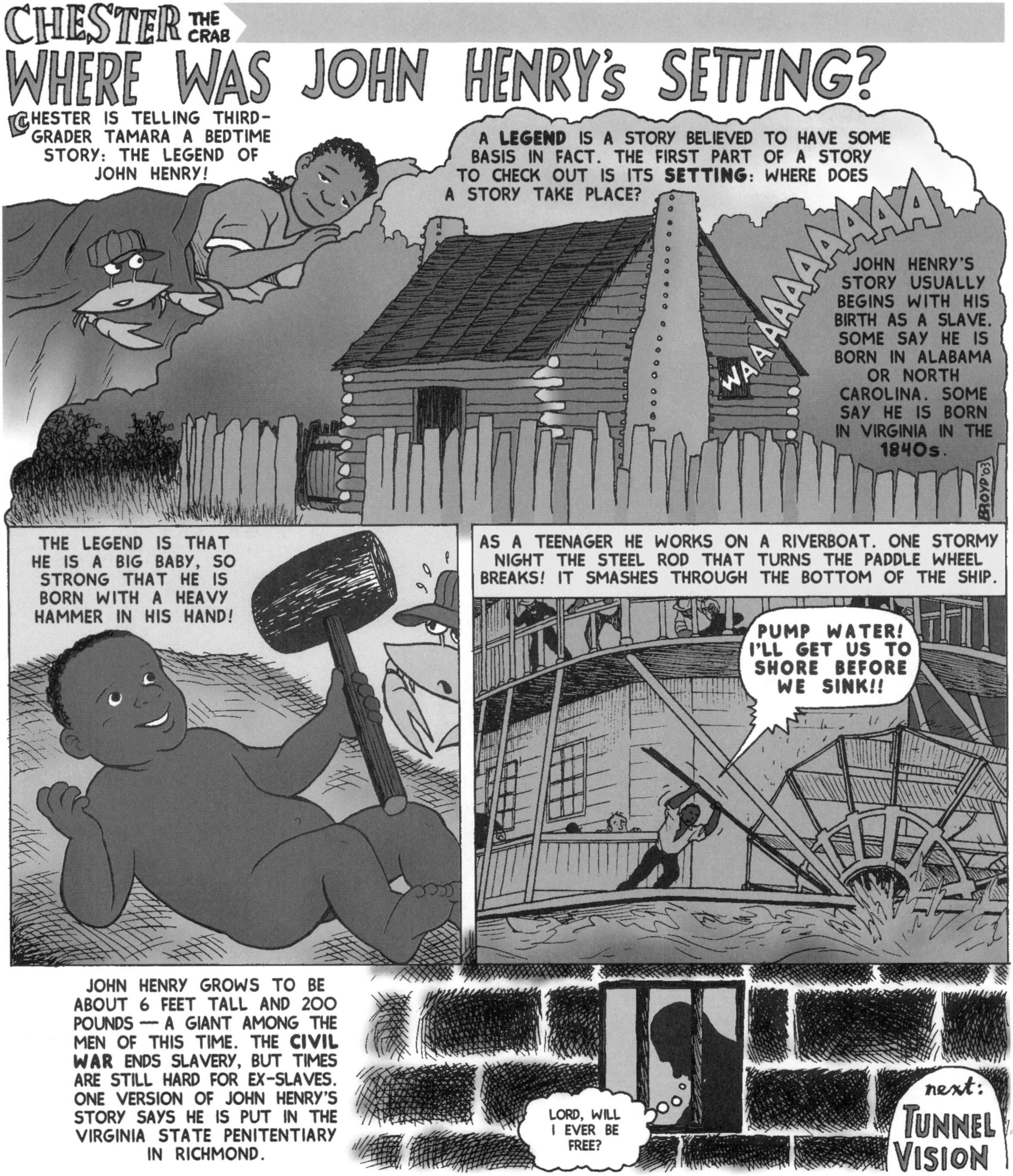
CHESTER THE CRAB
WHERE WAS JOHN HENRY's SETTING?
CHESTER IS TELLING THIRD-GRADER TAMARA A BEDTIME STORY: THE LEGEND OF JOHN HENRY!
A LEGEND IS A STORY BELIEVED TO HAVE SOME BASIS IN FACT. THE FIRST PART OF A STORY TO CHECK OUT IS ITS SETTING: WHERE DOES A STORY TAKE PLACE?
WAAAAAAAAAAA
JOHN HENRY'S STORY USUALLY BEGINS WITH HIS BIRTH AS A SLAVE. SOME SAY HE IS BORN IN ALABAMA OR NORTH CAROLINA. SOME SAY HE IS BORN IN VIRGINIA IN THE 1840s.
BOYD '03
THE LEGEND IS THAT HE IS A BIG BABY, SO STRONG THAT HE IS BORN WITH A HEAVY HAMMER IN HIS HAND!
AS A TEENAGER HE WORKS ON A RIVERBOAT. ONE STORMY NIGHT THE STEEL ROD THAT TURNS THE PADDLE WHEEL BREAKS! IT SMASHES THROUGH THE BOTTOM OF THE SHIP.
PUMP WATER! I'LL GET US TO SHORE BEFORE WE SINK!!
JOHN HENRY GROWS TO BE ABOUT 6 FEET TALL AND 200 POUNDS — A GIANT AMONG THE MEN OF THIS TIME. THE CIVIL WAR ENDS SLAVERY, BUT TIMES ARE STILL HARD FOR EX-SLAVES. ONE VERSION OF JOHN HENRY'S STORY SAYS HE IS PUT IN THE VIRGINIA STATE PENITENTIARY IN RICHMOND.
LORD, WILL I EVER BE FREE?
next: TUNNEL VISION

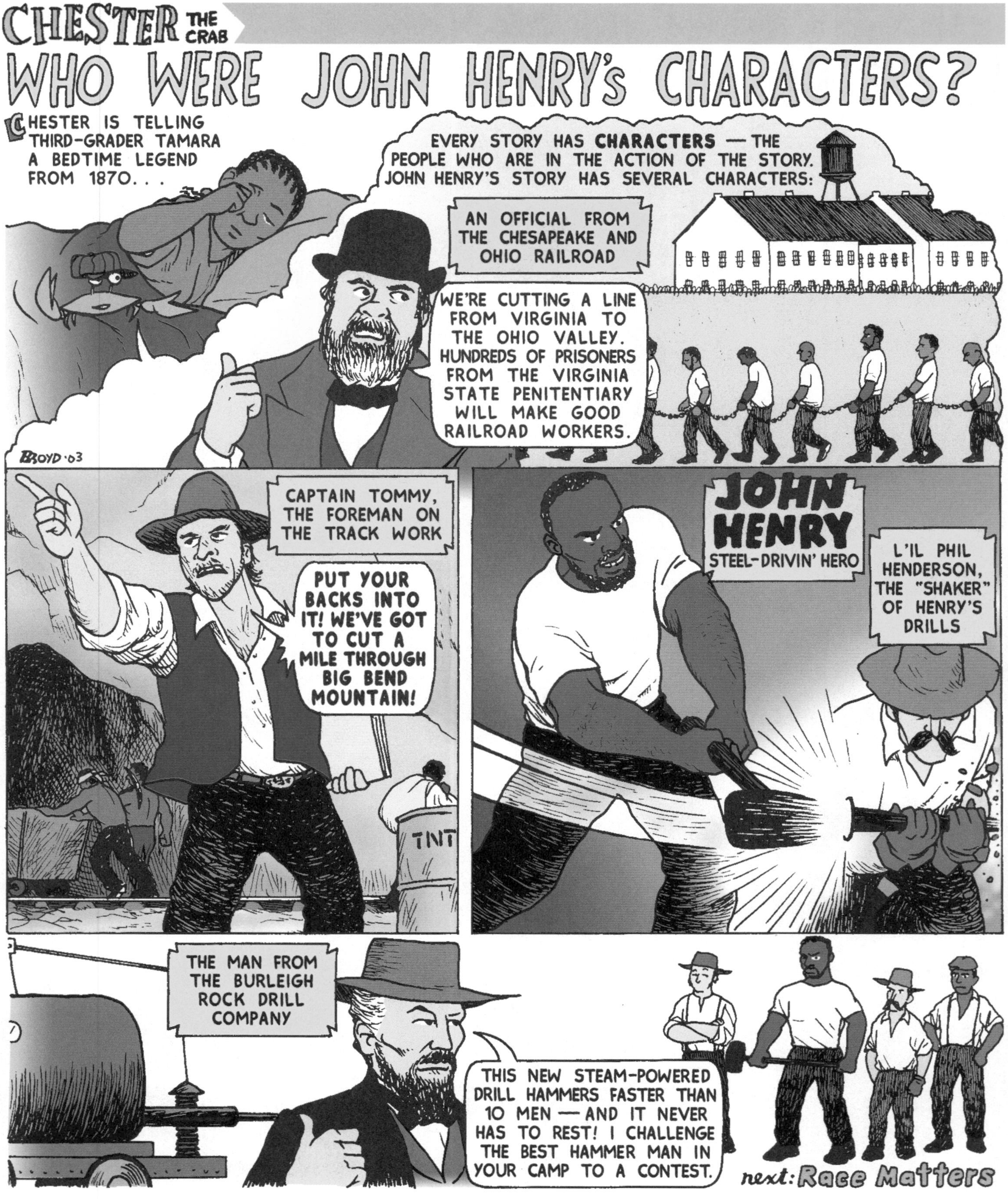
CHESTER THE CRAB
WHO WERE JOHN HENRY's CHARACTERS?
CHESTER IS TELLING THIRD-GRADER TAMARA A BEDTIME LEGEND FROM 1870. . .
EVERY STORY HAS CHARACTERS — THE PEOPLE WHO ARE IN THE ACTION OF THE STORY. JOHN HENRY'S STORY HAS SEVERAL CHARACTERS:
AN OFFICIAL FROM THE CHESAPEAKE AND OHIO RAILROAD
WE'RE CUTTING A LINE FROM VIRGINIA TO THE OHIO VALLEY. HUNDREDS OF PRISONERS FROM THE VIRGINIA STATE PENITENTIARY WILL MAKE GOOD RAILROAD WORKERS.
BROYD '03
CAPTAIN TOMMY, THE FOREMAN ON THE TRACK WORK
PUT YOUR BACKS INTO IT! WE'VE GOT TO CUT A MILE THROUGH BIG BEND MOUNTAIN!
TNT
JOHN HENRY
STEEL-DRIVIN' HERO
L'IL PHIL HENDERSON, THE "SHAKER" OF HENRY'S DRILLS
THE MAN FROM THE BURLEIGH ROCK DRILL COMPANY
THIS NEW STEAM-POWERED DRILL HAMMERS FASTER THAN 10 MEN — AND IT NEVER HAS TO REST! I CHALLENGE THE BEST HAMMER MAN IN YOUR CAMP TO A CONTEST.
next: Race Matters

CHESTER THE CRAB

HOW DID MUSIC MOVE JOHN HENRY?

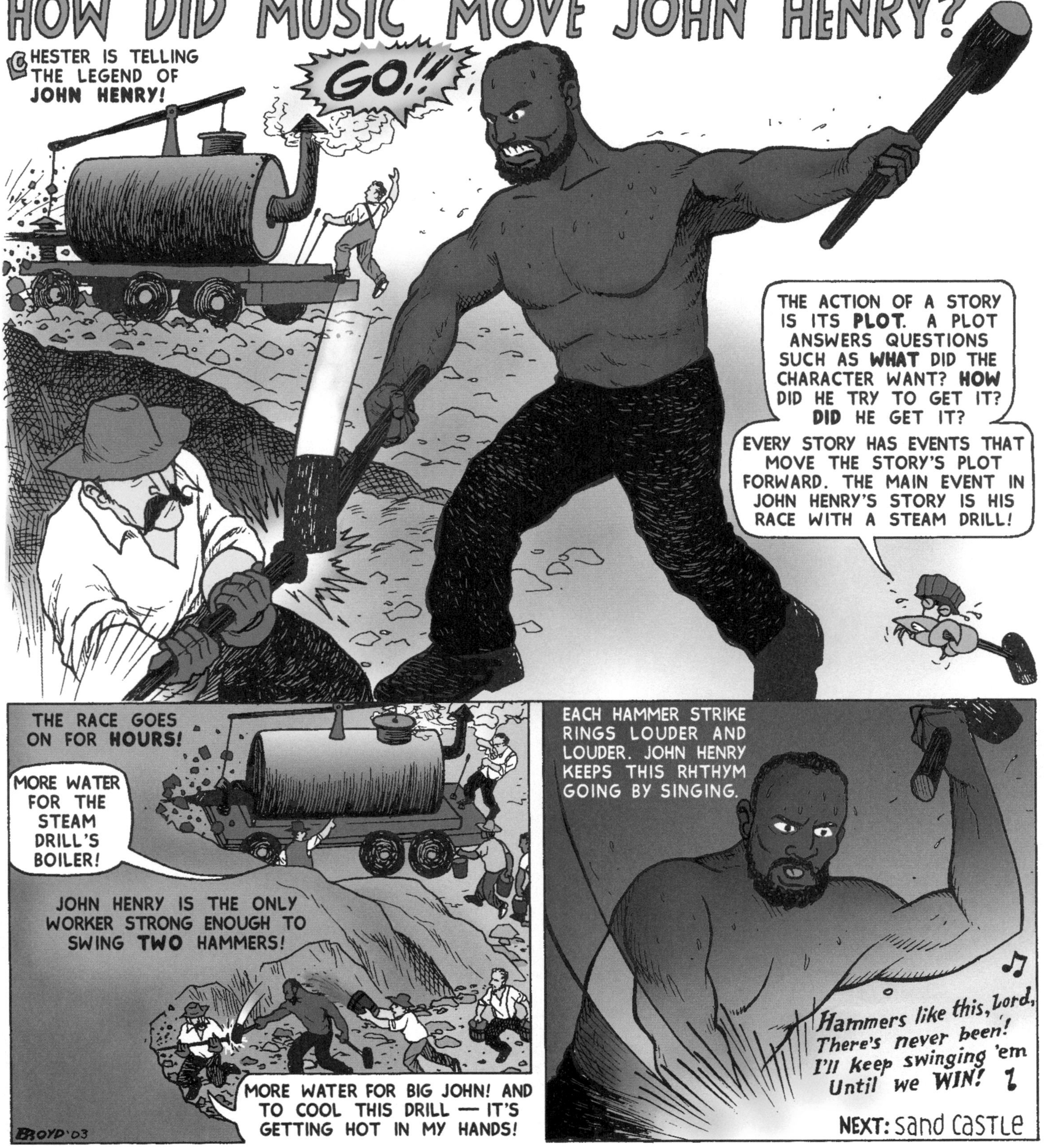
CHESTER IS TELLING THE LEGEND OF JOHN HENRY!
GO!!!
THE ACTION OF A STORY IS ITS PLOT. A PLOT ANSWERS QUESTIONS SUCH AS WHAT DID THE CHARACTER WANT? HOW DID HE TRY TO GET IT? DID HE GET IT?
EVERY STORY HAS EVENTS THAT MOVE THE STORY'S PLOT FORWARD. THE MAIN EVENT IN JOHN HENRY'S STORY IS HIS RACE WITH A STEAM DRILL!
THE RACE GOES ON FOR HOURS!
MORE WATER FOR THE STEAM DRILL'S BOILER!
JOHN HENRY IS THE ONLY WORKER STRONG ENOUGH TO SWING TWO HAMMERS!
MORE WATER FOR BIG JOHN! AND TO COOL THIS DRILL — IT'S GETTING HOT IN MY HANDS!
BOYD '03
EACH HAMMER STRIKE RINGS LOUDER AND LOUDER. JOHN HENRY KEEPS THIS RHTHYM GOING BY SINGING.
Hammers like this, Lord,
There's never been!
I'll keep swinging 'em
Until we WIN!
NEXT: Sand Castle

WHAT WAS JOHN HENRY'S CONCLUSION?

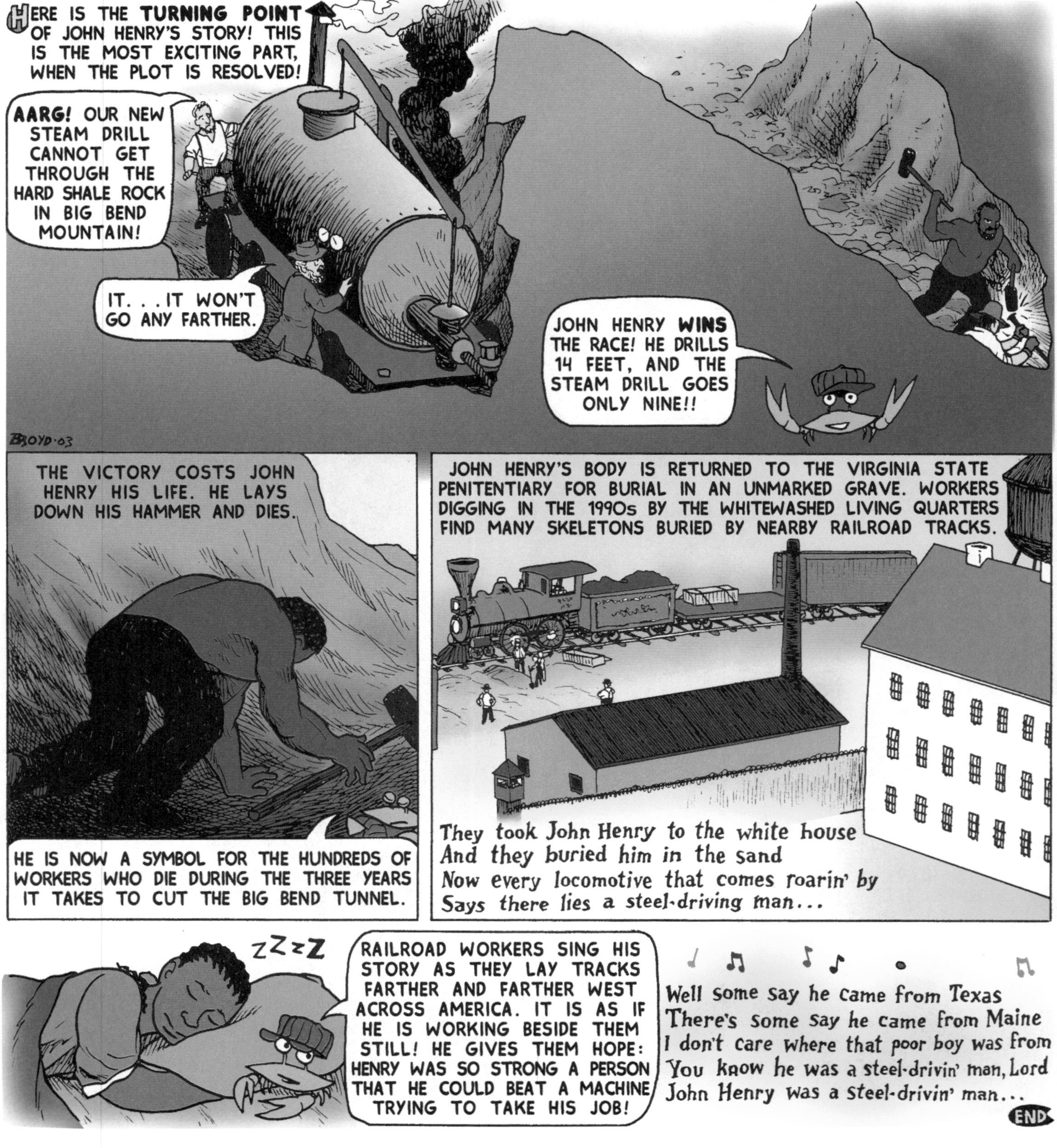

HERE IS THE **TURNING POINT** OF JOHN HENRY'S STORY! THIS IS THE MOST EXCITING PART, WHEN THE PLOT IS RESOLVED!

AARG! OUR NEW STEAM DRILL CANNOT GET THROUGH THE HARD SHALE ROCK IN BIG BEND MOUNTAIN!

IT. . .IT WON'T GO ANY FARTHER.

JOHN HENRY **WINS** THE RACE! HE DRILLS 14 FEET, AND THE STEAM DRILL GOES ONLY NINE!!

BBOYD·03

THE VICTORY COSTS JOHN HENRY HIS LIFE. HE LAYS DOWN HIS HAMMER AND DIES.

HE IS NOW A SYMBOL FOR THE HUNDREDS OF WORKERS WHO DIE DURING THE THREE YEARS IT TAKES TO CUT THE BIG BEND TUNNEL.

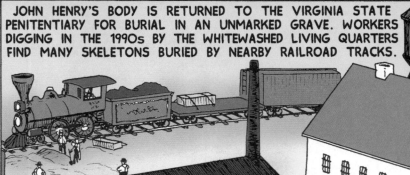

JOHN HENRY'S BODY IS RETURNED TO THE VIRGINIA STATE PENITENTIARY FOR BURIAL IN AN UNMARKED GRAVE. WORKERS DIGGING IN THE 1990s BY THE WHITEWASHED LIVING QUARTERS FIND MANY SKELETONS BURIED BY NEARBY RAILROAD TRACKS.

They took John Henry to the white house
And they buried him in the sand
Now every locomotive that comes roarin' by
Says there lies a steel-driving man...

RAILROAD WORKERS SING HIS STORY AS THEY LAY TRACKS FARTHER AND FARTHER WEST ACROSS AMERICA. IT IS AS IF HE IS WORKING BESIDE THEM STILL! HE GIVES THEM HOPE: HENRY WAS SO STRONG A PERSON THAT HE COULD BEAT A MACHINE TRYING TO TAKE HIS JOB!

Well some say he came from Texas
There's some say he came from Maine
I don't care where that poor boy was from
You know he was a steel-drivin' man, Lord
John Henry was a steel-drivin' man...

END